Dear Parent:

Congratulations! Your child is taking the first steps on an exciting journey. The destination? Independent reading!

STEP INTO READING® will help your child get there. The program offers five steps to reading success. Each step includes fun stories and colorful art. There are also Step into Reading Sticker Books, Step into Reading Math Readers, Step into Reading Write-In Readers, Step into Reading Phonics Readers, and Step into Reading Phonics First Steps! Boxed Sets—a complete literacy program with something for every child.

Learning to Read, Step by Step!

Ready to Read   Preschool–Kindergarten
• big type and easy words • rhyme and rhythm • picture clues
For children who know the alphabet and are eager to begin reading.

Reading with Help   Preschool–Grade 1
• basic vocabulary • short sentences • simple stories
For children who recognize familiar words and sound out new words with help.

Reading on Your Own   Grades 1–3
• engaging characters • easy-to-follow plots • popular topics
For children who are ready to read on their own.

Reading Paragraphs   Grades 2–3
• challenging vocabulary • short paragraphs • exciting stories
For newly independent readers who read simple sentences with confidence.

Ready for Chapters   Grades 2–4
• chapters • longer paragraphs • full-color art
For children who want to take the plunge into chapter books but still like colorful pictures.

STEP INTO READING® is designed to give every child a successful reading experience. The grade levels are only guides. Children can progress through the steps at their own speed, developing confidence in their reading, no matter what their grade.

Remember, a lifetime love of reading starts with a single step!

For my nieces and nephews—
Kate, Simon, Marinda, Joshua, Miriam,
Naomi, Isabelle, Sam, Rebecca, and Julie—
for whom Bell's talking machine
is a thing of the past
—M.K.

For Sarah, with love—R.N.W.

With grateful acknowledgment to Jim DeWalt of the Rare Book Department at the Free Library of Philadelphia and Sharon Morrow of the Alexander Graham Bell National Historic Site of Canada for their time and expertise in reviewing this book.

Photo credit: Alexander Graham Bell at the opening of the long-distance line from New York to Chicago in 1892 courtesy of the Library of Congress.

www.stepintoreading.com

Educators and librarians, for a variety of teaching tools, visit us at
www.randomhouse.com/teachers

Library of Congress Cataloging-in-Publication Data
Kulling, Monica.
Listen up! : Alexander Graham Bell's talking machine / by Monica Kulling ;
illustrated by Richard Walz. — 1st ed.
    p. cm. — (Step into reading. Step 3 book)
ISBN 978-0-375-83115-7 (trade) — ISBN 978-0-375-93115-4 (lib. bdg.)
1. Bell, Alexander Graham, 1847–1922—Juvenile literature. 2. Inventors—United States—Biography—Juvenile literature. 3. Telephone—History—Juvenile literature.
I. Title. II. Title: Alexander Graham Bell's talking machine.
TK6143.B4K85 2007
621.385092—dc22   2006021524

Printed in the United States of America

10 9 8 7 6 5 4 3 2 1

First Edition

LISTEN UP!
Alexander Graham Bell's Talking Machine

by Monica Kulling
illustrated by Richard Walz

Random House 🏠 New York

Arf! Arf! Arf!

"Come here, boy!"
Alexander Graham Bell
wanted to show
his brothers
a trick.

Scotland, 1857

4

He could stroke

the dog's throat

so that it sounded

like the dog was talking!

Alec's father
had taught him
all about sound.
"Sound moves
through the air in waves,"
said Papa.

"When the waves
hit your ear,
you hear the sound."

Alec loved sound.
He loved to sit
under the piano
and sing out loud.
His voice made
the piano wires shake!

When Alec grew up,
he still loved sound.
He also loved inventing.
Alec knew that sound
shook a wire.
Could it also cross *over* a wire?

Boston, 1874

If Alec could invent
a talking machine,
then people could talk
to each other—long-distance!

Alec knew how

he wanted

the talking machine to be.

But he did not

know how to build it.

He hired a young man
named Tom Watson.
Tom could build anything.
He built the two parts
of the talking machine.

The sending part
of the talking machine
had a mouthpiece
that looked like a cone.

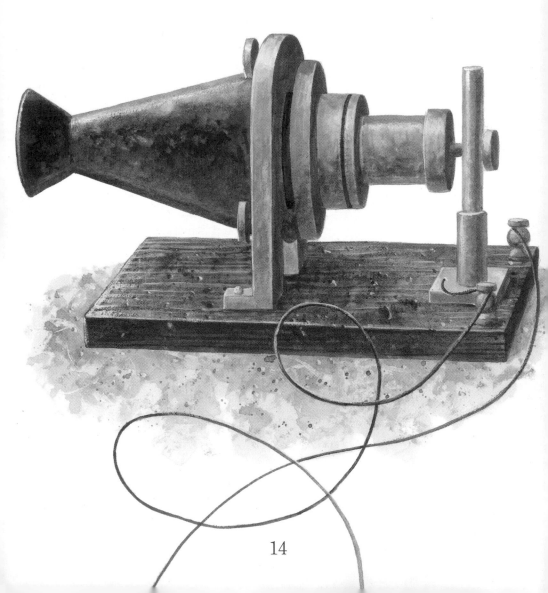

The receiving part
was in another room.
The two parts
were joined by a wire.
The wire was connected
to a battery.

When Alec spoke
into the cone,
the battery sent out
waves of electricity.
In the other room
Tom listened,
but heard nothing.
Alec and Tom worked hard.

They tried many ways
to make the machine work.
But every time
Alec spoke into the cone,
Tom heard nothing.

Then one day
they tried something new.
This time when Alec spoke,
Tom came running.

"Did you hear what I said?"
asked Alec, excited.
"No," said Tom.
"But I *did* hear
the rise and fall
of your voice!"

One day,
by accident Alec spilled
acid on his pants.
He called into the cone,
"Watson, come here!
I want to see you."

Watson came running.

"It works! It works!"

he shouted.

"I heard every word!"

Chug! Chug! Chug!
Alec was going
to Philadelphia.
He was taking
his talking machine
to the World's Fair.

Philadelphia, 1876

22

The United States
was 100 years old!
There were parties
everywhere.
The World's Fair
was the biggest party of all.

Excitement
was in the air.
The whole world
had come to visit
the fair!
Alec didn't know
what to do first.
He might visit
the Egyptian mummy.

Or stroll through
the sweet-smelling
Japanese garden.

Or listen to
the musical clocks.

It was a world
of wonders!

A giant steam engine
powered lights
and elevators at the fair.
People were filled
with awe
to see it working.

A pickle salesman
named Henry Heinz
had made
a new tomato sauce.
He called it ketchup.

Soon restaurants
all over America
would have bottles
of ketchup
on their tables.

Charles Hires had made

a drink from roots.

He called it root beer.

It was a hot summer day.

Alec bought a bottle.

Yum!

There were many
interesting inventions
at the fair.
The typewriter.

The sewing machine.

The calculator.

Alec's talking machine
was in a corner
up a flight of stairs.
It was too hot.
No one wanted
to climb the stairs.

Alec was worried.
What if no one
saw his invention?

But one person *did*

climb the stairs.

He was Dom Pedro,

the emperor of Brazil.

"What is this thing?"

he asked.

"Let me show you," said Alec.

Dom Pedro held
the hearing piece
to his ear.

On the other side
of the building,
Alec spoke into the cone:
"To be or not to be . . ."
The room was noisy.

But Dom Pedro
heard Alec's voice,
loud and clear.
Dom Pedro
dropped the hearing piece.
"It talks!" he shouted.

People wanted
to know why Dom Pedro
was so excited.
The judges lined up
to try the machine.
They couldn't believe
that you could talk
to someone
across a crowded room
without shouting.

They were convinced.
Alec's talking machine
was a marvel!

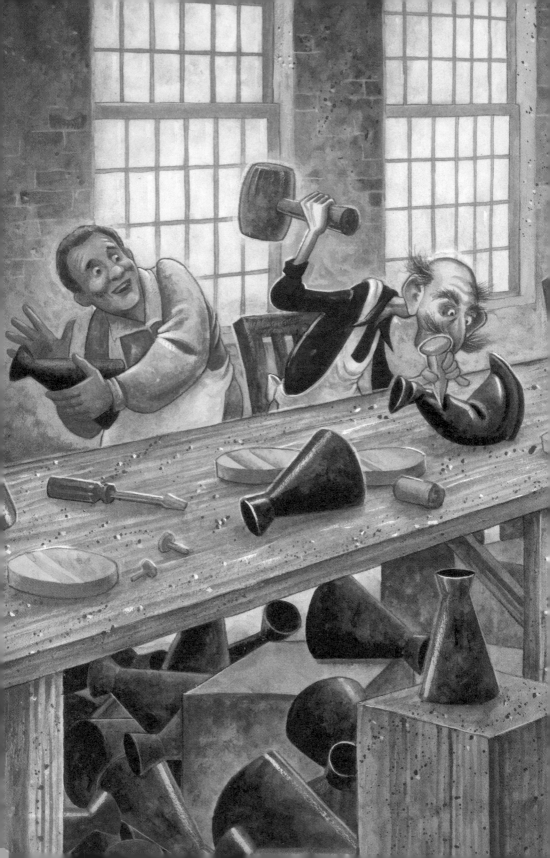

Alec called his invention
the telephone,
which means "far talking."
Soon telephones
were being made
all over the world!

At first, people
were afraid of
the telephone.
It might
spread disease!

Everyone would
know their business!
Life would never
be the same!

But in time,
people grew to love
the telephone.
You could talk
to a friend far away.

Or phone the doctor
if you were sick.

Or buy groceries
without leaving
your house!

Alec and Watson loved
to show people
their invention.
Brrriiing!
"Hoy! Hoy!" shouted Alec
into the receiver.

The audience watched
while Alec spoke
to Watson in a city
over twenty miles away.

Alexander Graham Bell was famous for that first phone call at the World's Fair. People often told him, "The telephone will change the world." They were right.

Here is a photo of Bell using his talking machine in 1892.

AUTHOR'S NOTE: The stories in this book are true. We can't be sure *exactly* how they all happened, but we've tried our best to show the way things might have been.